Alan Fletcher

Contents

Words into Visions: Fletcher's Poetic Eye

I have known Alan Fletcher for very many years but we had not been in touch for quite a while when out of the blue (or orange or deep purple) a *special delivery* parcel arrived. First a stout cardboard box ideally dimensioned for the contents: 374 proof pages of this book, pages two and three left waiting for a preface which he was evidently expecting me to write. This message was conveyed in a perfunctory but rather charming letter: five lines from the computer but with a handwritten F and A enticingly aligned. Unpacking the box of colour proofs was a sheer pleasure. Alan had made a fairly firm request seem like a present, the whole transaction carried out with an offhand perfectionism characteristic both of Alan and his work.

Writers love Fletcher's art because it is so verbal. I tend to regard him as a writer manqué. We are both in the business of waiting for the moment of crystallization, when an idea changes state. The point at which the word transforms itself to make a picture. The stage at which the visual image claims an intellectual meaning. Fletcher, with his innate contrariness, likes reversing accepted designations and watching the results. If you call a pear an apple is it any longer pear-shaped? He plays games that stretch our verbal and visual perceptions. The name he gives them – 'graphic foibles' – is nice but not quite adequate. These are dazzling exercises in design philosophy.

As a small boy growing up in London he tells us how he noticed that the railings in the streets were not simply iron railings but an array of regularly spaced spears with decorative spearheads, strange and beautiful, like weapons of fierce exotic warriors. Fletcher looks hard at one thing and it leads him to another. Is that tagliatelle or is it shredded paper? Are those black olives or are they splats of ink? His work bears a sense of secret harmonies and magical progressions that seems to me to link him back to Karel Teige and the Poetismus movement of the Czech avant garde.

He is also very streetwise. Having studied at Yale and worked in New York in the late fifties his work has a quasi-American kind of urban knowingness, a love of puns and wisecracks. Fletcher is a fast mover, observing and detecting with the manic energy of a movie speeded up. He is endlessly resourceful. Stuck in a traffic jam he would improve the shining hour by amassing examples of street traders' calligraphy, marvelling at the geometry of markers in the road.

He is deeply interested in histories and narratives. This is another overlap between Fletcher the graphic artist and the novelist or biographer. He is adept at producing quick-fire portraits of people glimpsed in transit, in a city or an airport, drawing out their tribal attributes, ancestral characters. Fletcher's own physiognomy and stance marks him out to me as a member of the tribe who annexed London in the early 1960s. Eduardo Paolozzi, Enzo Apicella, Len Deighton, David Bailey, Terence Conran: these were people who altered Britain's visual culture and opened out a whole generation's cognisance of pleasure. Alan Fletcher's greed for experience, like theirs, had its origins in the austerities of wartime childhood. His besottedness with colour, the refulgent colours of the sunrise, counteracted the drab Britain of the post-war years.

This new book has a sense of glorious release. Much of his life's work has been involved with corporate design. Fletcher is now at liberty to thrill himself, testing out what you can do with the 26 letters of the alphabet, investigating variations of the ampersand, pursuing what Nabokov called 'the tactile delights of precise delineation'. There are multitudes of ways of looking at a palm tree. Welcome to Alan Fletcher in his palm tree days.

Fiona MacCarthy

Working and Playing

In 1956, as a recent graduate of the Royal College of Art, Alan Fletcher negotiated his escape to the United States of America. Following a time spent as a student at Yale School of Art under prominent teachers including Paul Rand and Josef Albers, he freelanced first in Los Angeles for the celebrated film title designer Saul Bass and later in New York for Leo Lionni, the art director of *Fortune* magazine. When he returned to England in 1959, he brought back with him the foundations of contemporary British graphic design. He had an impeccable CV and a portfolio of colourful work, the like of which his peers in frugal London hadn't a hope of emulating. More importantly, he had a newly ambitious understanding of the potential of design: its ability to engage and inform, to tease and amuse, and to confront and challenge. Working with the cream of America's professionals, he had learnt that the best graphic design connects with what people already know at the same time as rendering that knowledge utterly new and fresh.

Reflection combined with transformation has been the basis of Fletcher's method for the last half century. It gave his work from the 1950s a unique, witty hook, and it continues to be apparent on every page of this book. Each one of his drawings, collages, quotes, puns and plays reveal curiosity about the world combined with a will to remake it. Very little escapes Fletcher's attention and his desire, part profound, part impish, to turn things on their head (or on their side). Graphic design is a magpie discipline, and Fletcher is one of the sharpest eyed, greediest birds of them all. His influences are multiple and various: among them the Dadaist and Futurist's loose ways with letters, their play with typographic form and expression; the blank refusal of face value of the Surrealists; and, on a more formal level, the embrace of popular graphic codes by the painter Stuart Davis or the witty reworking of the ordinary by the illustrator Saul Steinberg.

Not only has Fletcher worked for over fifty years, he has worked hard for all that time. He has never made much of the struggle and sweat involved in either the creative or economic processes of graphic design, yet he has built up a vast archive of brilliant, influential work. Writing about his oeuvre, I often feel that I am making heavy weather of it, particularly in contrast with the lightness of the work itself. Sometimes it seems as if my labours will suppress its spirit, but at these moments I summon up the common wisdom: looking easy is the very hardest thing to achieve. Anyone who has seen the marked-up proof copy of Fletcher's magnum opus *The Art of Looking Sideways* can be in no doubt of the level and extent of the designer's application. With coloured tags signalling corrections on what must be every other page, this work-in-progress demonstrates just how painstaking, painful even, that progress can be.

These days Fletcher is based in a studio in one of London's loveliest mews. The overall impression of the space is light, white and airy, yet it is filled with objects: pieces of design, totems, curios, souvenirs and novelties. Some of them I recognize from photographs of Fletcher's workspaces taken in the mid-1960s, while others I know to be recent presents from admiring younger designers. The studio is connected to Fletcher's house and his transition between life and work is seamless. Spending time in Fletcher's easy company, you could think that he was never at work. The truth is, he is never away from it.

Building on the contradictory constants of work and play, Fletcher's life can be explored in terms of a series of tensions and balances. His affection for the old combined with his love of the new, for example. I believe that Fletcher is a modernist, he aims to improve our lives through design, yet his modernism is of a particularly pragmatic, maybe particularly British, make-do-and-mend kind. When he bought his first mews house in the early 1960s he scraped what he could from the brick walls and painted the rest white. The result was a bright, new environment cased in a Victorian brick shell. The effect was enhanced by the combination of iconic modern furniture, Eames loungers and Bertoia mesh chairs, and a salvaged wrought-iron staircase.

Fletcher is absolutely a man of his time – the product of 1950s New York and 1960s London, the 1970s and 1980s international corporate environment, a 1990s desire for simplicity and a millennial urge for revelation – yet this is far too reductive an account for someone who has maintained a consistent point of view for over half a century. There are Fletcher collages dating from the 1950s that could have been made yesterday, and there are logos, such as that for the V&A, which manage the seemingly impossible trick of being in tune with the era of their design while still looking fresh decades after their inception.

Another tension, and one that is very pertinent here, lies between what is for us and what is for him. The work in this book came about through Fletcher's perpetual curiosity and desire to create. Now it is available for our consumption, but well before this book came about, some of it had made its way into other professional jobs, greetings cards, calendars and the like. Some of it even began life as a commission, for instance Fletcher began drawing the facades of buildings as a means of injecting some much needed joy into the design for a programme of international medical conferences. When Fletcher was part of Pentagram, the design consultancy he helped found in 1972 and worked at for the next twenty years, he had to generate enough income to keep his team running. One of his former assistants, Paul Anthony, compares it to running a kindergarten. A period of responsibility and no little stress, these were the only years of Fletcher's career that he laboured in anything like a conventional sense. These days, he works to please himself, and we're lucky enough that sometimes some of it makes its way into the public eye.

Latterly, Fletcher has become known for his elegant and distinctive handwriting, the intermittently interlocking characters that snake their way through so much of his work. Looking back through his work from the 1970s and 1980s, however, I was surprised to find how little of his stroke was visible. Similarly, he produced some beautiful drawings in the 1950s, but then spent the next thirty years commissioning illustrations from others while barely doing a doodle for professional purposes. In 'Words into Visions: Fletcher's Poetic Eye', the preface to this volume, Fiona MacCarthy calls the last ten years Fletcher's 'palm-tree days'. You could go further and invoke the notion of a full circle. To posit a final tension, and embrace a cliché, although much of this book seems to be the work of an instant, it is, of course, the product of a lifetime.

Emily King

PLEASE REMOVE
RABBIT
BEFORE HANDING
IN HAT

People and Places

Once upon a time Adam and Eve lived in
Eden, although in different places and times.
In the anthropological story they never met.

However, ecclesiastics will be relieved to
learn that a scientific genetic analysis, which
included Australian aborigines, Danish
housewives and Patagonian indians, indicates
that every single living person is descended
from one ancestral African Eve who lived
around some 150,000 years ago.

When travelling I usually carry a notebook.
These are some of the ancestral characters
I've seen in terminals, boardrooms, cafés,
pubs, bars, hotel lobbies, planes and trains,
at conferences and on beaches.

Clockwise (top left): Tokyo, Delhi, Bodrum, London

Clockwise (top left): Heathrow, St Barts, Camps Bay, Malmö

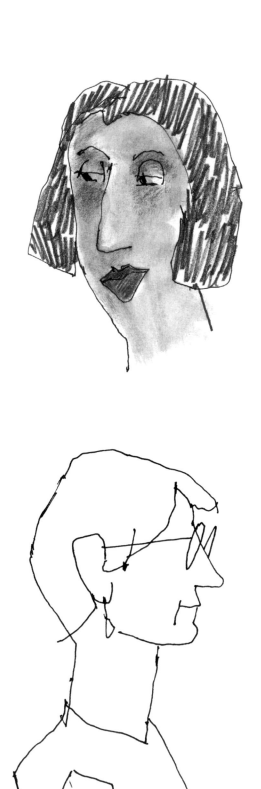

Clockwise (top left): Venice, Istanbul, Bedarra, Budapest

Clockwise (top left): Budapest, Capetown, Monterey, Holetown

The six degrees of separation

There is a theory that we are only six hand-shakes away from meeting anybody in the world. You would like to meet Madonna or Maradona? No problem.

The theory was originally devised by a Harvard psychologist who sent letters to 300 people in Omaha, asking them, through their personal contacts, to forward the letter to a single named person in Boston. For various reasons only 60 letters reached their target, but the average number of steps taken of those which did, was six.

David Hampton short-circuited the theory by posing as the son of movie star Sidney Poitier. A ruse that led to a lifetime of infamy conning wealthy Manhattanites out of thousands of dollars, and providing the story for the play *Six Degrees of Separation*.

What are you?

Are we merely assemblies made up of previous personalities, laid down like rock strata over time? A jigsaw layer of genes in which the pieces for each generation have fallen, or have been arranged, in one kind of pattern? A sum total of everybody we have ever been?

The answer must be 'yes'. As geneticist JBS Haldane remarked, he would happily lay down his life for eight of his cousins, since between them they possessed more of his genes than he did.

Typographic Folk Art

The letters used in these compositions were retrieved from abandoned market cartons, graphic ephemera and other printed rubbish.

Cleating a variety of poorly printed materials, with disparate and unrelated letter forms, into cohesive graphic arrangements is no easy task.

First you have to find the letter. Say the curly C of the Coca-Cola logotype. Retrieve the carton, discreetly cut out the letter, get rid of the carton, soak the piece of card in water (Third World boiled-bones glue makes it difficult to separate paper from card), peel off the printed sheet, lay it out to dry.

Assembled into a new context, the letters can now spell out different statements or messages. Or indulge in word play.

I think of them as font refugees from the civic garbage-disposal unit.

I found these letters in the market.

Word pictures

Letters form words that convey meanings that can make pictures.

These compositions illustrate SHAPES, one LINE, and some SHADE.

An alert eye

The opportunities and potentials lying within a word are generally not recognized. Here are some that were.

The ubiquitous EVIAN mineral water carton aptly translates palindromically into French. REVERSE and BALANCE do just that. STUPID is assembled from bits and pieces.

As Mae West remarked, it is better to be looked over than overlooked.

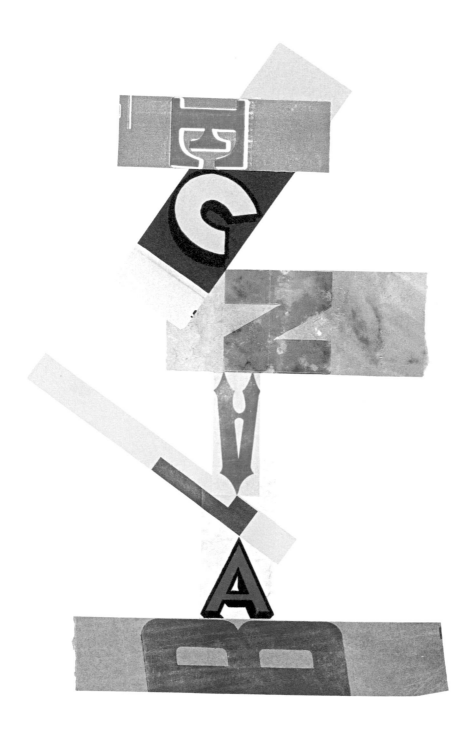

Ambiguity

Art critic Brian Sewell was asked which living artist he would least like to be stuck in an elevator with. 'Tracey Emin,' he replied, 'with a full bladder.' I'm not sure whether he meant his or hers.

FE Smith (renowned newspaper proprietor and later peer) used to nip into the Athenaeum, of which he was not a member, to use their loo on his way to the House of Lords. After complaints from members, the porter pointed out to him that the club was for members only. 'Sorry,' Smith replied, 'is it a club as well?'

The painter Augustus John was less ambiguous when a society matron asked him: 'Would you like to paint me naked, Mr John?' 'Very much, madam. Just the socks on.' 'Socks, Mr John?' 'Somewhere to keep my brushes, madam.'

Shared opinion

'The tactile delights of precise delineation, the silent paradise of the camera lucida, and the precision of poetry in taxonomic description represent the artistic side of the thrill which accumulation of new knowledge, absolutely useless to the layman, gives its first begetter... There is no science without fancy, and no art without facts.'

Vladimir Nabokov
Strong Opinions, Weidenfeld and Nicholson (London 1974)

Menagerie of Imaginary Creatures

These creatures were born to amuse my
three-year-old grandson on holiday. His task
was to collect the rubbish. Mine was to
make something of it.

The first creature took shape with the core
of a toilet roll, four corks, a piece of card, two
bottle tops. All stuck together, covered with
papier mâché and bright red poster paint.

As I was handing him the finished article, with
instant recall I remembered that Paul Klee
always knew when something was finished
because instead of him looking at the subject,
the subject began looking at him.

With great presence of mind I suggested to
my grandson that he gave the creature a name
and sound, while I would look after it. He
thought that was a good deal and is happy
with the arrangement.

A whimsical menagerie soon followed,
conjured up from plastic spoons, bits of string,
cigarette cartons, drawing pins, clothes pegs,
ribbons, wires. Dressed in newsprint and
daubed with colour.

And here, by grace of God and presence
of mind, are most of them.

Fido
045

Hooligan
046

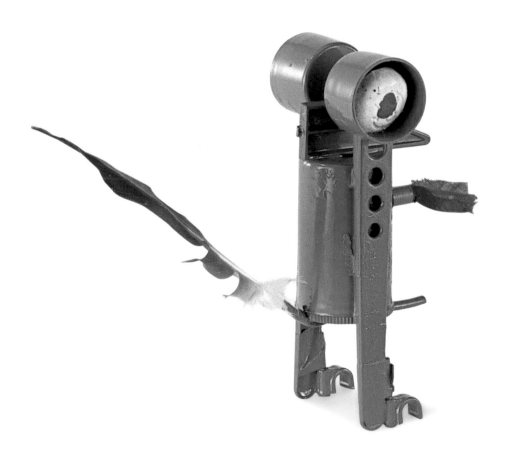

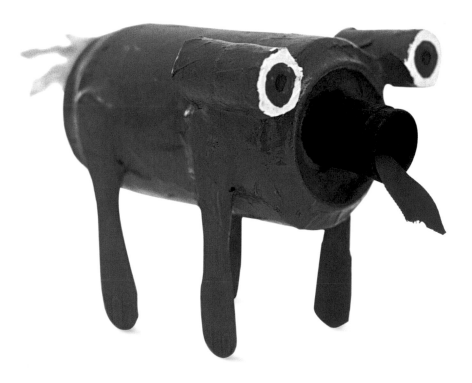

Bouncer
053

Gbobledigook Rlues OK

Orus is the age of sbusttiutes: isntead of lagnuage, we hvae jragon; intsaed of pirncpiles, solgans; and insetad of gneuine iedas, Birght Idaes. Eirc Bnetley mdae a btiter obsrevation alnog thsee lnies in the *Nwe Rpeublic* bcak in 1952. Eevn he mghit have been apapiled to dicsover that, just hlaf a cnetury laetr, our brians would hvee leraned to do whtiout acucrate spleling too.

Yet that appaers to be the csae. Resaerch by a Cmabrigde lnagugae and raeding epxert, Dr Rsoaleen McCrathy, sugegsts taht we can udnrestnad any wirtten text, howveer mnagled, as long as the frist and lsat lteters of ecah wrod are in the rghit palce. Taht ptus piad to the shcool of thuoght that we raed lteter by letetr. It sgugests insetad taht our barins practcise a mroe sohpistciated from of ptatern recogintion with wrods, maknig it piotnless to work too hrad at odrering eevry letetr crroectly.

This is gald nwes for delniqeunt or dylsexic spellres eevywhree, from molesworth senoir (the cruse of st csutards) to Dan Qauyle. But it wlil, equlaly, srtike trreor into the haerts of eidtors aruond the ltierary wolrd, whsoe wroking lfie has been sepnt leraning the pianful task of idnetifying the rgoue typo or the senaky spleling erorr and shwoing the dveiants no mrecy. What does the ftuure hlod for these domoed suols, if splleing has smiply sotpped mattenirg?

Ocne releived of their day jbos mssaaging aawy now-ivnisible textaul infelciities, the wrodsimths of yseterday wlil, at laest, have tmie to pnoder the chnages in mdoern lfie that bruoght aubot tihs sdduen rdeundacny.

Moible phnoe texitng, with taht anonying auotmatic-seplling funtcion that 'crorects' all atetmpts to wirte "hello" itno nnosense wrods endnig wtih a qeustion mrak and an agrgieved electornic squeak, must be the vlilain of the peice. Who wolud ever hvae raelized that the presice intrenal configiurations of a word maent so ltitle witohut bieng focred to inteprret hrruied comumnicatoins raeding "hlo onwayhmoe" or scary abberviations such as "cul8er" or "iluvu"? Comemrcial cmoptuter porgrammes are relpete with ohter vritual vlilains – Wrods dteerminedly do-godoing Mr Ppaercilp is one – whsoe prupose is to do all the thniking for the user, laeving huamn pratners in the buisness of wrtiing hapiply idle, infnatilized and incerasingly illtierate.

Yet three may be wodnerful appilcations of our nelwy dicsovered lignuistic flexbiility. Chuacer's archiac, radnomly splet wrok has tromented chlidren since wriitng was satndardized. But there is lttile to fear now from pharses such as 'O stormy peple! Unsad and ever untrewe!' Prehaps it is tmie to trun the txteing gnereation losoe on the calssics agian.

The Times
23 September 2003

Alphabetic Excursions

I like things that express what they say. And
DRAWING has a particular opportunity to do
what it says.

The 26 characters of the ALPHABET can be
monogrammed to create all kinds of galaxies.
Like the stars at night, some monograms might
suggest mythical creatures, others a diagram
of a Cubist painting or merely demonstrate
geometric callisthenics.

The photograph, shown opposite, suggests
they could even be an educational tree.

Wondering how that ancient Greek decorative
device, the MEANDER, might just do that,
I had a notion that there would be a calculable
number of permutations.

Of course there is. It's called the Moonshine
Conjecture. I'm told it comes to 808,017,424,
794,512,875,886,459,904,961,710,757,005,754,
368,000,000,000. In addition there are all
the styles and techniques in which the letters
can be drawn.

Drawings of DRAWING

In drawing the seven letters of the word no rules were followed. The only constraint was to create an entity by superimposition and preserve the recognition value of each letter.

The drawings could have ranged in style from the severely geometric to frivolously free-form. However, these are my first tentative efforts to see where I was going. They show, I think, a naivety not so easy to capture with a more calculated approach.

So here they are.

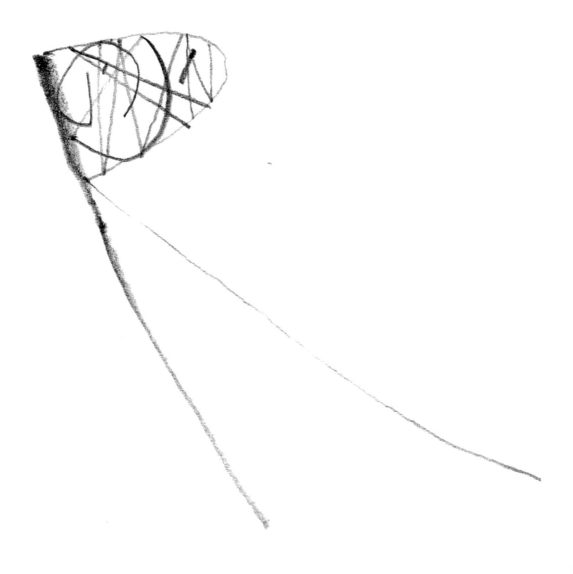

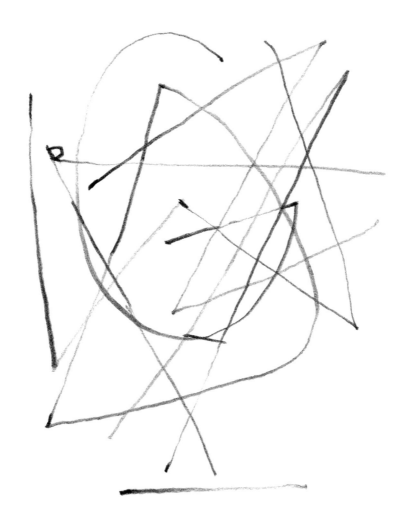

ALPHABET monograms

In idle moments some whittle wood, others build cathedrals with matchsticks. I tend to doodle.

Converting the 26 letters of the ALPHABET into clusters and galaxies has occupied many such moments.

I originally drew these monograms in pencil and then fiddled with them on my computer. They looked adequate, but lacked that extra something or other. Then I imagined how they might appear fashioned in that ancient artwork material called scraperboard, also known as scratchboard.

The result looks warmer than an unrelenting computer line. Don't you think?

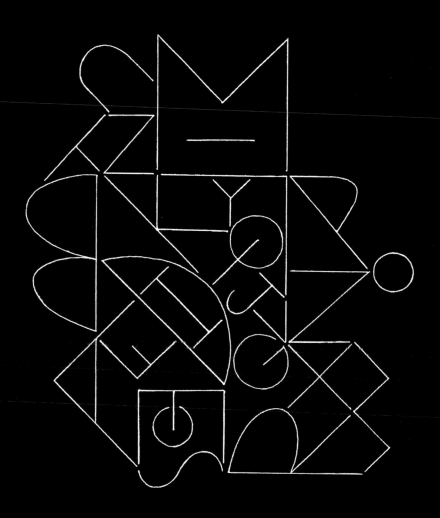

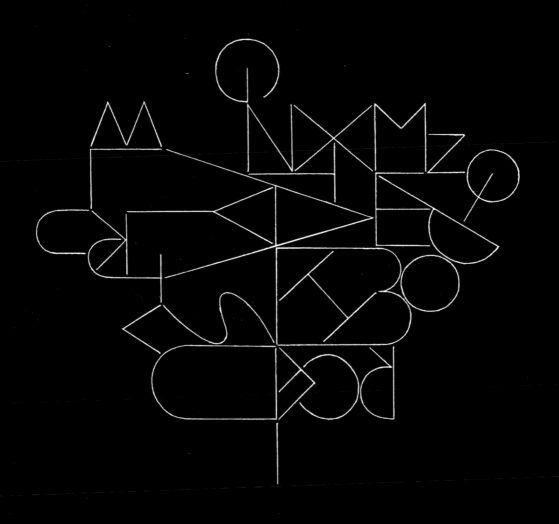

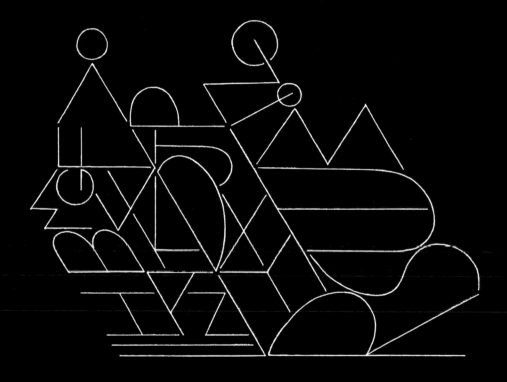

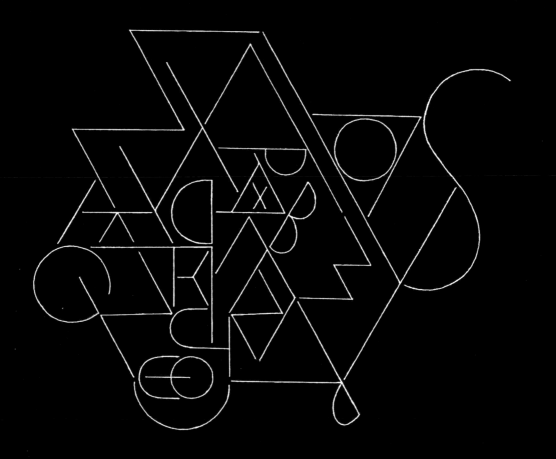

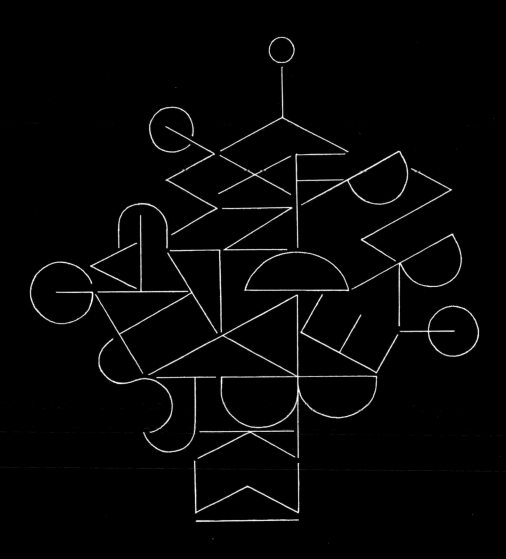

The MEANDER

The MEANDER follows several self-imposed
rules. The word can meander any which way
but must follow the alphabetic A to Z sequence.
Letters are allowed to ligature. That is to
say, share a line as in the illustration opposite.
They must connect with the previous and
following letter.

The lesson I learnt after producing several
dozen was that I could spend a lifetime without
ever repeating myself.

I stopped.

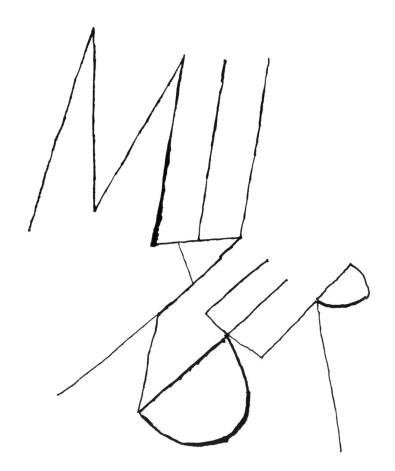

You are obliged to go off at a tangent if you want to stop going round in circles.

Forethought

'When I was working for the ad agency Leo Burnett in Hong Kong my managing director there was always hanging out with local policemen. So I got to hear quite a number of crime stories.

'The Hong Kong police had finally captured the youth leader of the Triads, the Hong Kong version of the Cosa Nostra. They locked him in a holding cell in the 20-storey police headquarters in Kowloon and questioned him for days without being able to extract any kind of information out of him. After hours and hours of unsuccessful questioning they completely lost it, grabbed him by his feet and hung him out of an 18th floor window. Still he would not talk.

'They had to set him free. He then turned around and sued the police department for applying torture during questioning. At the trial it was his word against that of five policemen, who all denied the charges. But he said he had proof. While they hung him out the window he had signed his name on the wall. And sure enough when the court went to check, there was his signature on the wall, written upside down 18 storeys up in the air.'

Stefan Sagmeister
Design Indaba Magazine (Winter 2006)

Who Was Who

These rudimentary sketches, retrieved from my notebooks, record meals with colleagues and friends. Since I have zero skill at conjuring likeness, I write in names so as to remember who was who. The writing is therefore part of the picture.

The instruments are pens, pencils, fingers, water, red wine, espresso dregs and sediment from Greek coffee. Sometimes tomato sauce, vinegar and olive oil are called on to contribute.

One reason to do the sketches is to record memories of friends and pleasurable times. But the real reason is I like doing them.

my

Jerome

Peter

Rupert

Yumble

...h @ Glynn-Smiths   19/VIII

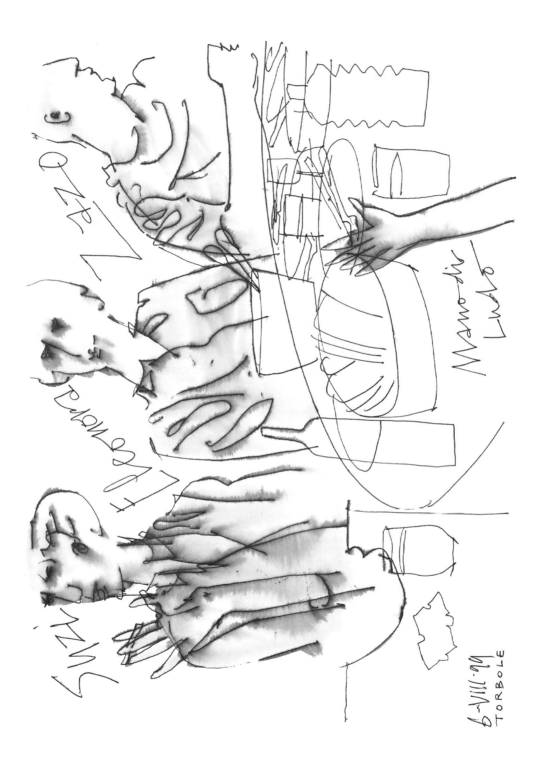

Kostas.
Stelios
Paola
Dimitris
Supper in Thessaloniki at the home of Delislis. Marians 26/6/04
Michael
Atiki
Stergiafis Freddie
Agnes

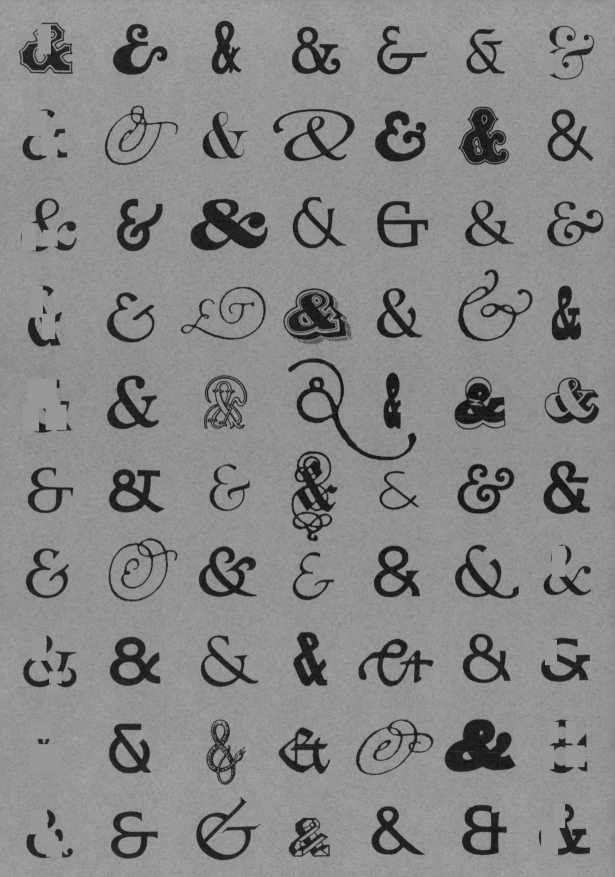

Badger Graphics

Badgers come in setts. I must have learnt this from a book in childhood, since, being a city dweller, I'm not aware I've ever seen a badger. Anyway, the term 'sett' indicates that although badgers look similar, each has an individual character.

You can also spell the term 'set' with one 't'. By the way, the *Oxford English Dictionary* (bumper edition) lists 430 definitions of this term and, so here is another one. Of course, a cynic might consider badger graphics mere repetition, the definition of cliché.

Actual size detail of Vagabond Pizza (version 2)

Vagabond Pizza

These pizzas are assembled with labels, stickers, price tags and endorsements surreptitiously acquired by the author on shopping trips or sent by friends around the world.

Although running a blue ballpoint around a kitchen plate and sticking down such stuff appears an innocent occupation, the pizzas also have their sinister aspect. For instance, they reveal the contributors' personal eating habits, reflect their financial spend and indicate social standing.

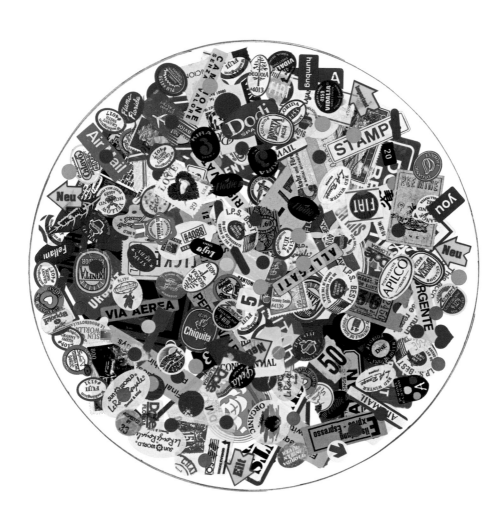

Vagabond Pizza (version 2)

Vagabond Pizza (version 6)

Vagabond Pizza (version 9)

Observations on art

This is an assembly of observations on art by 30 illustrious luminaries from Oscar Wilde to Susan Sontag.

Each comment is handwritten, one on top of the other. Although, metaphorically, they are all talking at once, the noisy result is an artistic comment in itself.

Observations on art by Friedrich Schiller, Pablo Picasso, Paul Standard, Adolf Loos, George Ivanovitch Gurdjieff, James Joyce, Émile Zola, Alfred Jarry, Herbert Read, Louis Sullivan, Lionel Trilling, Oscar Wilde, Ambrose Bierce, Francisco de Goya, Eugene Delacroix, Henri Matisse, Heraclitus, JMW Turner, Walter Pater, Vladimir Mayakovski, Renen Hughe, Jean Anouilh, Peter Ustinov, Edwin Lutyens, GK Chesterton, Al Capp, Frank Auerbach, Maurice Denis, Anaïs Nin, Francis Bacon, Saul Bellow, Edgar Degas, Susan Sontag, John Singer Sargent, Marshall McLuhan, Ernst Gombrich, Al Álvarez, WH Auden, Bernard Berenson, William Blake.

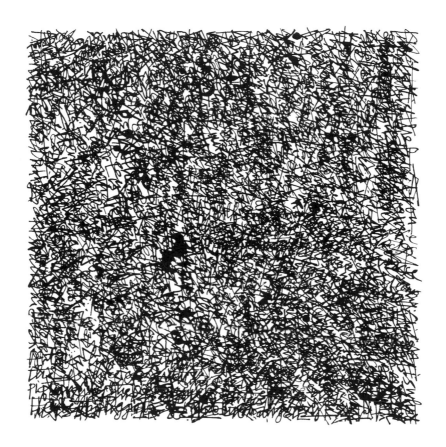

Soft lead pencil

The campus fountain

These are three wood models from a collection of 12 drinking fountains designed to stand in the streets and public spaces of a new campus being built for a large pharmaceutical company to house administration and laboratories.

They will stand one metre high and each will be made in a different coloured stone.

The shapes of the fountains will be silhouette profiles of 12 famous cultural figures.

The conundrum of whether you see either the positive or negative of a shape or form has long fascinated the perceptual psychologist.

The three fountains shown here are of Albert Einstein, Le Corbusier and Carl Gustav Jung.

Albert Einstein looking at Albert Einstein

Carl Gustav Jung looking at Carl Gustav Jung
105

Nonsense diagrams

Social scientists, marketing agencies and gossip columnists set great store by relationships revealed by interconnections.

These diagrams of connections don't present a statistical conclusion or fulfil a function. They merely diagram diagramming. Nevertheless, there is a visual pleasure in the weave of warp and weft in the pattern.

Pleasure also fulfils a function.

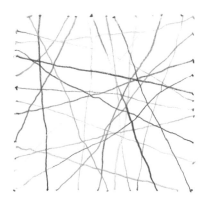

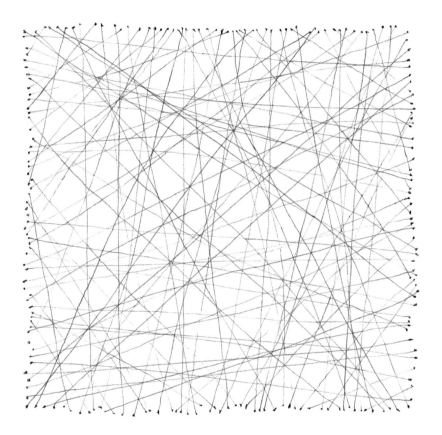

Four doppelgängers

One report which has persisted is that Saddam deployed 16 lookalikes throughout Iraq. By the time the war was over, there were only 12 left. 'We got rid of four,' one source put it metaphorically when under interrogation. Anyway, here are four of them relaxing off duty.

Santa Claus

The name Santa Claus comes from the Dutch
word Sinterklaas, aka Sint Nikolaas, aka Saint
Nicholas, a fourth century Turkish holy man.

During Christmas Santa Claus really gets about.
He is everywhere seemingly at the same time.
In department stores, shopping malls, streets,
markets, fairs and events.

Have you also noticed that although he looks
the same, he isn't? Sometimes he wears
spectacles, other times not. Sometimes he's
tall, other times short, full of bonhomie, or
tired and grumpy.

Anyway, my Santa Claus is always the same
except for his expressions. I show him as
he appeared on a set of Christmas cards. You
could select his demeanour and mood to
match that of the person to whom you were
sending the card.

'There are flowers everywhere, for those who
bother to look.'

Henri Matisse

Dust to dust

'Fling your arms wide in an expansive gesture to span all of evolution from its origin at your left fingertip to today at your right fingertip. All the way across your midline to well past your right shoulder, life consists of nothing but bacteria. Many-celled, invertebrate life flowers somewhere around your right elbow. The dinosaurs originate in the middle of your right palm, and go extinct around your last fingerjoint. The whole story of *Homo sapiens* and our predecessor *Homo erectus* contained in the thickness of one nail-clipping.

'As for recorded history; as for the Sumerians, the Babylonians, the Jewish patriarchs, the dynasties of Pharaohs, the legions of Rome, the Christian Fathers, the Laws of the Medes and Persians which never change; as for Troy and the Greeks, Helen and Achilles and Agamemnon dead; as for Napoleon and Hitler, the Beatles and Bill Clinton, they and everyone that knew them are blown away in the dust from one light stroke of a nail-file.'

Richard Dawkins
Unweaving the Rainbow, Penguin (London 1998)

Wild Flowers

These imaginary blooms are a blend of watercolour and chance.

Real flowers have two Latin names. One is the family name, the other the given name. They also have nicknames like daisy and dandelion.

Anyway, these wild flowers have also been given Latin names. They were derived by purchasing a book on botany, extracting the index, slicing the pages vertically in half, and sliding one half up against the other – then reading off the pairs.

So when your knowledgeable gardener nods wisely, permit yourself an inward smile.

Spotted Rockrose. *Caldesia maritima*

Field Fleawort. *Achilles alpinus*

Downy Woundwort. *Dancus alisma*

Whorled Water-milfoil. *Callitriche palustris*

Stinking Helebore. *Bupleurum orientalis*

Ragged Robin. *Calystegia palustris*

Cornish Fumitory. *Armeria humifusa*

Lesser Twayblade. *Glancium sylvaticum*

The African embassy myth

When I was a small boy my uncle told me you could always recognize an African embassy in London because the blades of the railings outside the building were painted in gold. I was enchanted. It was then that I also realized that railings were an array of regularly spaced spears and not just a boring assembly of pointy rails.

Entranced, this information remained a truism in my mind for decades. The other week, out for a stroll, I decided to check out the railings of a few African embassies. Not one of them had gold blades. I was deeply disappointed.

So much for received wisdom.

But I learnt something else. The humble blade comes in a multitude of shapes and forms.

Railings seen and photographed by Leah Klein.

Relics

'The Morgan library in New York has a very fine eleventh-century Lancelot in perfect condition. I was going over it one day and turned to the rubric of the first known owner dated 1221, the rubric a squiggle of very thick ink. I put a glass on it and there imbedded deep in the ink was the finest crab louse, *Pfithira pulus*, I ever saw. He was perfectly preserved even to his little claws.'

John Steinbeck
Elaine Steinbeck and Robert Wallsten (eds), *Steinbeck: A Life in Letters*, Heinemann (London 1975)

'I have a small drawing by Klee on which, if you look closely, you can see a hair – from his mustache or eyebrow, it's hard to tell – embedded in the ink ever since it was liquid. And so I, too have my relic: a hair of Klee.'

Saul Steinberg
Reflections and Shadows, Allen Lane (London 2002)

The Zodiac

Illustrations of the zodiac are invariably of the cute, sentimental and cloying throw-up variety. The images here take a different tack and just rely on cut paper shapes with a minimal inkpen line or two.

Judging from newspapers and magazines, readers are devotees of the zodiac.

Even psychologist and philosopher Carl Gustav Jung believed in astrology. He once compared the birth signs of happily married pairs with those of divorced couples. The results, he claimed, revealed that those favourably matched were more likely to have permanent wedded bliss.

Which one of these is your match?

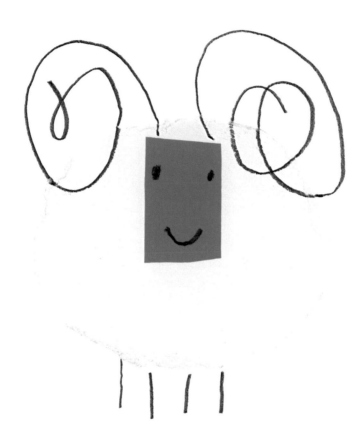

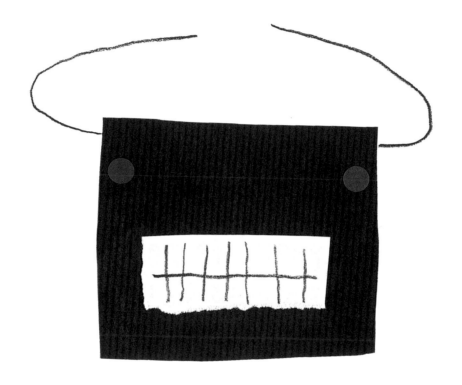

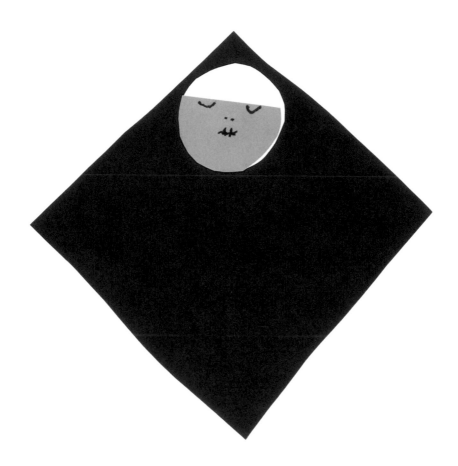

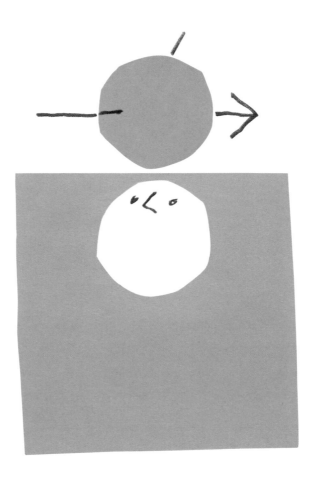

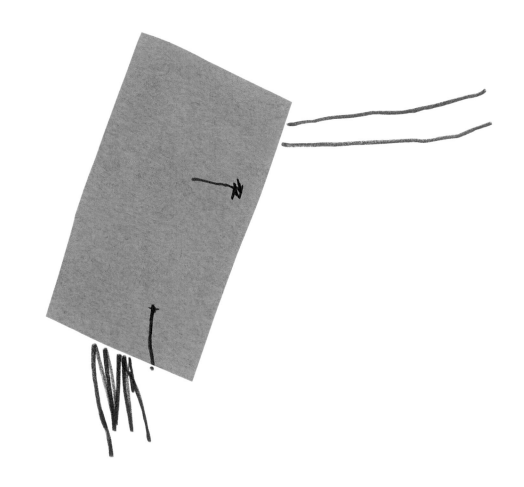

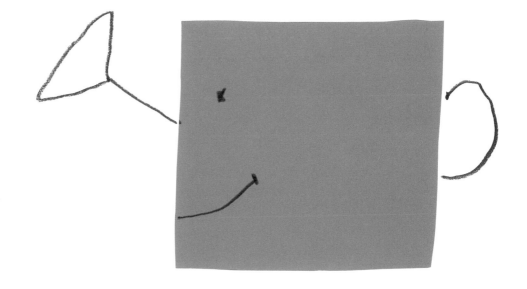

'In architecture form is a noun;
in industry form is a verb.'

Buckminster Fuller

The square

'The square is as high and as wide as a man with his arms outstretched. In the most ancient writings, and in the rock inscriptions of early man, it signifies the idea of enclosure, of house, of settlement.

'Enigmatic in its simplicity, in the monotonous repetition of four equal sides and four equal angles, it creates a series of interesting figures: a whole group of harmonic rectangles, the golden section, and the logarithmic spiral, which also occurs in nature in the organic growth of plants and in parts of animals.

'With its structural possibilities it has helped artists and architects of all epochs and styles by giving them a harmonic skeleton on which to build an artistic construction.'

Bruno Munari
Discovery of the Square, Tiranti (London 1965)

Squaring Up

Apart from so-called Word Squares, like the Latin one illustrated below and a contemporary version opposite, there is often no logical reason to use a square field.

'Form follows function' is the maxim quoted by your reductionist. Well so it does. But as Casanova may well have proposed – function also follows form.

When I'm stuck with a sticky visual problem I confess I follow the latter principle. My approach is quite simple. How can I make this design work within a square?

For example the construction of an S-Type Jaguar from the pages of its catalogue or the assembly of features for an unlucky zombie.

S	A	T	O	R
A	R	E	P	O
T	E	N	E	T
O	P	E	R	A
R	O	T	A	S

S-Type Jaguar

A speech

'From the pictures sent in for exhibition it is clear that the eye of some men shows them things other than as they are – that there really are men who on principle feel meadows to be blue, the heavens green, the clouds sulphur-yellow ... Either these "artists" do really see things in this way and believe in that which they represent – then one has but to ask how the defect in vision arose, and if it is hereditary the Minister of the Interior will have to see to it that so ghastly a defect shall not be allowed to perpetuate itself – or, if they do not believe in the reality of such impressions but seek on other grounds to impose them upon the nation, then it is a matter for a criminal court.'

Adolf Hitler
Extract from a speech delivered at the inauguration of the House of German Art, Munich, 1937

Crossed wires

Anne Fadiman, author of *Ex Libris*, writes that she feels Sophocles is terracotta, Proust is dove grey, Conrad is cinnamon, Wilde is acid green, Poe is Prussian blue, Auden is indigo, and Roald Dahl is mauve.

Synaesthetes get their sensory wires crossed. They feel shapes, smell noises, see flavours, and hear colours. Liszt, Wagner, Scriabin ('D major was yellow') and Goethe all saw musical notes in colours. For Anthony Burgess an oboe was 'silver-green lemon juice' and a flute 'light brown and cold veal gravy'. 'Absolute green' for Wassily Kandinsky was the placid middle notes of a violin. And the writer Rimbaud felt that the letter A was 'a black hairy corset of loud flies'.

This description of a beach near Stintino in Sardinia conveys the idea.

A twisted new moon of luminous coral sand meets a clear shallow sea in an uproar of blue. Cyan, aquamarine, amethyst, cobalt, cerulean, violet, indigo, turquoise, lapis lazuli, lavender. It is astonishing, the optical equivalent of the cymbals being clashed beside your ear. It is so blue, when you look at it your skull feels hollow. It is like sucking a lemon.

A condition well-expressed by Oscar Wilde's comment: 'Only a deafman could wear a tie like that.'

Colourways

Art curator Harald Szeeman spoke English, German, French and Italian. 'Excuse me Harald,' I once asked, 'which language do you dream in?' 'Black and white,' he replied.

Colour is relative – that is to say your notion of what is red may not be mine. When I look at a blue sky over a green field you might – in my terms – be seeing a yellow sky over a violet field.

Even if we share the same colour sense we don't share the same colour sensitivity. Ask ten people to give you a swatch of red and you'll receive ten different shades of red.

Giving different colours different names doesn't automatically clarify matters.

A word symbolises whatever it represents. So if I state this is PINK you expect to see something pink. If what you see labelled is sludge green you would resonably assume it is either the wrong word or the wrong colour.

But, actually, that's only your point of view.

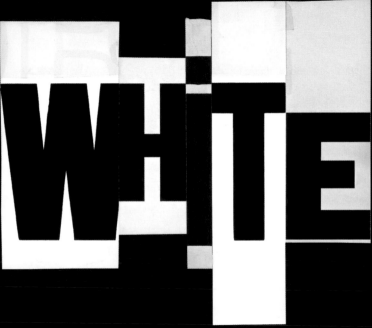

Faces seen and photographed by François and Jean Robert

Visual Comparisons

I'm told there's a proverb that states there is more than one way to bake a parrot — a quaint way of saying one can look at things in lots of different ways.

one's not
half two—
it's two
are halves
of one.

E pluribus unum

Young man

Old man
177

Ink olives

Paper tagliatelle
179

A splodge

A one-liner

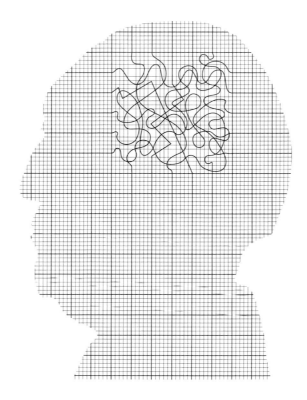

Deep thoughts

Pencil tree

I found the branches for this tree on a beach

Project for a weather vane
186

Louise thinking, listening and laughing. 11/3/03

A hello/goodbye one-liner wave

A design recipe

'Game is absurdly cheap. Our household gets through 150 head a year, but some City flakes suppose that it is acceptable to kill birds without eating them.

'After a shoot the other day, Caroline Tisdall of the Countryside Alliance staged a game-cookery demo to promote sales. Clarissa Dickson Wright taught us a trick I have never seen before.

'Place a feathered pheasant on the floor and stand astride it, one foot on each wing. Then take the legs in both hands and pull firmly but steadily. One is left holding simply the skinned breast on the bone. This is much easier than plucking.'

Maxwell Hastings
The Spectator, 14 February 2005

The ortolan

Shortly before his death in 1996, former French president François Mitterand had supper with friends. Each diner was presented with a roasted ortolan. A tiny bird the size of a lemon.

The president and his guests placed napkins over their heads and bent over their dish to inhale its delicate vapours and aromas. They then took the bird by its beak and sucked out the innards and bones, through its rectum.

A subject of medieval poetry, the endangered little bunting is regarded by French gourmets as the world's greatest delicacy. Towards the end of summer, migrating birds were trapped in small cages hidden among the branches of trees. Once captured, ortolans were force-fed for three days with grain and grapes. Then drowned in slugs of cognac before being prepared for table. Another recipe advocates asphyxiation by immersing their heads in very strong vinegar.

Authorities have now banned ortolan hunting.

Carton Icons

The image opposite portrays a pessimist. The umbrella forever open anticipating the rain. Tautological arrow requiring verbal reassurance. The fragile glass.

These three ubiquitous icons appear on cartons and packing cases. Their message hovering between description, command and reference.

They exist all over the world and appear in a multitude of colours, sizes, styles, shapes and forms. They are the epitome of a universal pictorial language.

Uncomfortable with conformity, I relish the thought that in different contexts such icons can be manipulated to convey alternative meanings.

Here are some ideas in that direction.

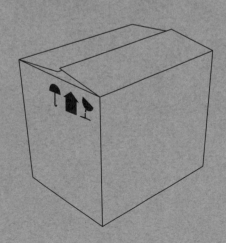

picture of a pessimist

Umbrellas

The open brolly can provide protection or
an environment for the other icons. Brollies
come in all sorts of sizes and shapes. Each
lending themselves to one interpretation
or another. As you can see in the picture
opposite in one circumstance the arrow, in
addition to directing, can also adopt the
role of wind or rain.

Optimist and pessimist

The conundrum of whether a glass is half full or half empty, and its corollary of optimist and pessimist, can be expressed by combining two different versions of a glass.

And not necessarily assembling them in the standard manner of half full at the bottom and empty at the top.

You have no idea how difficult it is to find two glasses to fit neatly together as these. Glasses appear in a myriad of shapes, sizes, colours and forms as indicated by the three examples shown below.

The paper carrying the glasses is folded and not cut.

Cocktails

Mixing, folding and combining various coloured glasses can create combinations reminiscent of exotic cocktails.

Salutations

Every time I clink a celebratory glass, the possibility of a disastrous situation flashes across my mind.

Luckily, so far, it has never happened.

Confrontations

The arrow is either lethal, directional or confrontational.

The following arrangements could be viewed as military front lines, domestic conflict, corporate takeovers or hostile encounters.

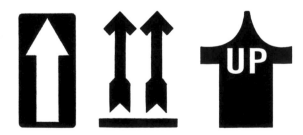

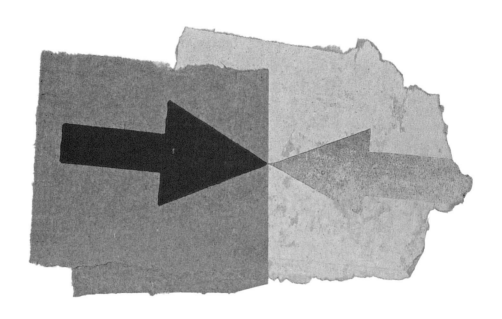

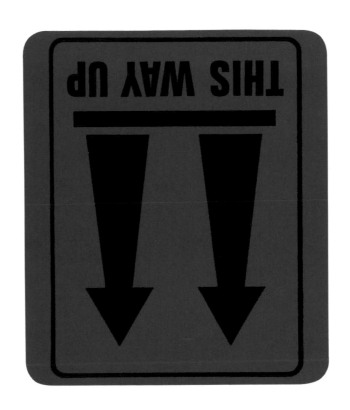

DOWN WITH DOGMA

Origami

I've heard of someone who knows someone
who does reverse origami. His favourite piece
is to grab a swan by its neck and in a few
deft and dextrous moves unfold it into a large
sheet of white paper.

Useful hint

'About 25 species of sharks are dangerous.
Sharks will not attack unless provoked. Face
and watch quietly any shark that is acting
aggressively and be prepared to push it away
with a camera, knife or tank. If someone is
bitten by a shark, stop the bleeding, reassure
the patient, treat for shock and seek immediate
medical aid.'

James Lyon
Maldives, Lonely Planet Guides (London 2003)

Billet Doux

A pseudo-scientific line of enquiry into the realm of graphic absurdity. These notes demonstrate the influence of context, action and topography on handwriting.

Actually, these are not just casual scribbles gratuitously abandoning control to the unpredictable results of haste. The aim was to exercise as much control as possible in adverse circumstances.

Writing in a taxi driving jerkily up a frenetically busy street. Writing while walking quickly, writing walking barefoot, under a hot midday sun on a gravel path. Writing while walking backwards up a street in the drizzle with eyes closed.

So what's the point? I've no idea. But I find the results are often an entertaining visual surprise. And one doesn't encounter those too frequently.

I'm a right handed person. [Written with my left hand.]

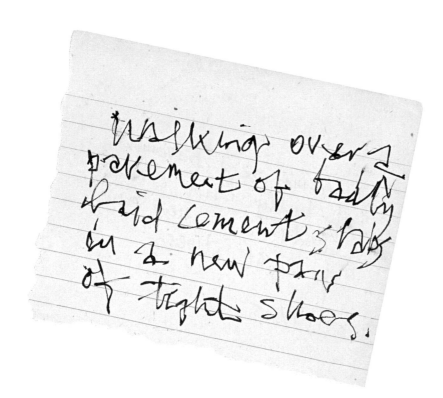

Walking over a pavement of badly laid cement slabs in a new pair of tight shoes.

Eyes closed. Writing holding [guiding] my left hand with my right.

Wheels hit the tarmac in BA 555
landing at Heathrow

19/2/03

Wheels hit the tarmac in BA 555 landing at Heathrow.

Writing with my eyes shut and feeling extremely bored, Basle airport about 5.30pm on Wednesday evening the 1st of January 2003.

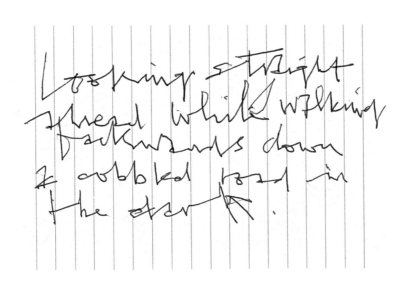

Looking straight ahead while walking backwards down a cobbled road in the dark.

I'm going to stick this note in a puddle.
227

Crime is only
a left-handed
form of human
endeavour

An artifact

'Consider a mug of American coffee. It is found everywhere. It can be made by anyone. It's cheap – and refills are free. Being largely without flavour it can be diluted to taste. What it lacks in allure it makes up in size. It is the most democratic method ever devised for introducing caffeine into human beings.

'Now take a cup of Italian espresso. It requires expensive equipment. Price-to-volume ratio is outrageous, suggesting indifference to the consumer and ignorance of the market. The aesthetic satisfaction accessory to the beverage far outweighs its metabolic impact.

'It is not a drink, it is an artifact.'

Tony Judt
The Spectator, 10 February 2005

The maker

'In classical Greek, the idea of the "artist" is covered by several words, all of which carry the sense of skill, manufacture, technique, expertise, etc. *Demiourgos*, "one who works for the people", might be used for cooks as well as for sculptors.

'The first meaning of *poietes* was "maker". TS Eliot would have been a *poietes* who made poems. I drag him in because *The Waste Land* was dedicated to "the better maker" (*il miglior fabbro*) – Ezra Pound – and that's a notion of art I understand. I grew up with it. As with poets, so with artists.

'From Praxiteles to Pollock (not to stop there), the artist was somebody who made something.'

Tom Stoppard
'Making It', *Times Literary Supplement*, 15 June 2001

The Chinese Horoscope

According to legend, Buddah once invited all the animals to join him in celebrating the New Year. Only 12 came. Naturally the rat was the first and the pig the last. To thank and honour his guests, he named a different year after each animal. Henceforth, anyone born in that year would acquire the animal's characteristics.

And so the Chinese horoscope was founded.

I have been collecting printed ephemera for years: tickets to a memorable exhibition, baggage stickers for a trip to America, an envelope from a kind letter, my first vehicle licence (page 239). The sort of material that holds meanings for me and nobody else.

A palette for constructing the animals.

Working with these materials each animal had to be brought to life. However, to up the stakes I restricted the imagery to heads.

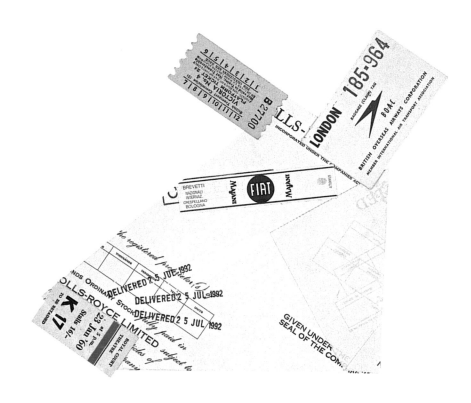

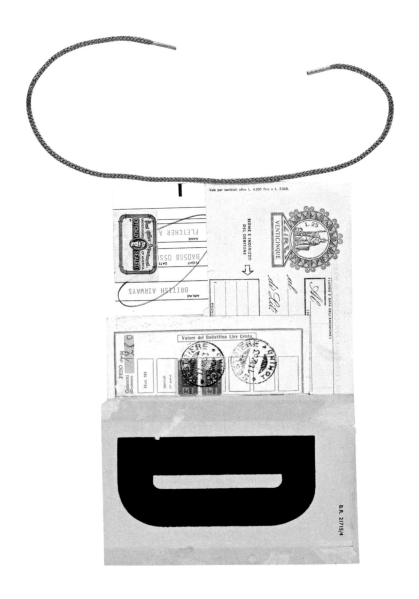

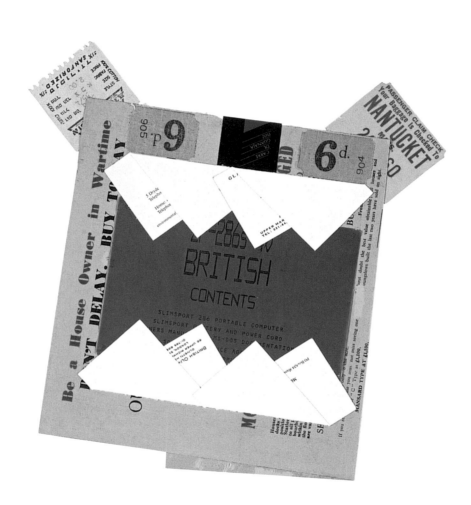

Year of the Tiger (based on Tipu's Tiger)
235

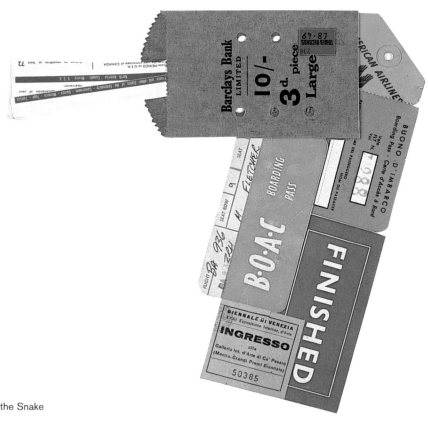

'There are three arts – painting, music and ornamental pastry-making; of the last, architecture is a subdivision.'

A pastry cook

The status factor

An exhibition of South American art displayed an Inca shirt covered with a decorative pattern of 156 miniature shirt designs. These were assembled in rows to form one overall master design. The person entitled to wear this must have been socially superior to all the lesser shirt-wearers whose miniaturized designs were incorporated into his. A hierarchical concept which not only visually declared a status but also produced a beautiful pattern.

The inevitable question is did function lead and beauty follow? Or vice versa?

Less inevitable is the better question. Why can't function be beautiful?

Marilyn's French curves

These curves were traced by Japanese architect Arata Isozaki from photographs of Marilyn Monroe. He uses them in his designs. He gave this set of their silhouette stencils to designer Ron Arad. And Ron Arad lent them to me so I could trace off the contours. Now you too can do designs like Arata Isozaki and Ron Arad.

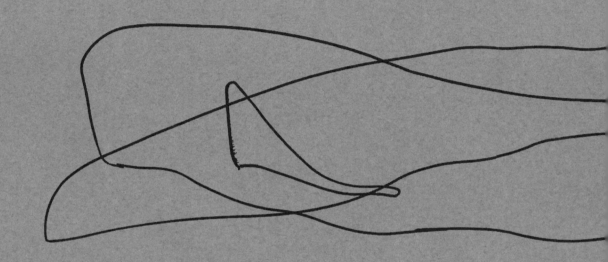

A commercial French curve

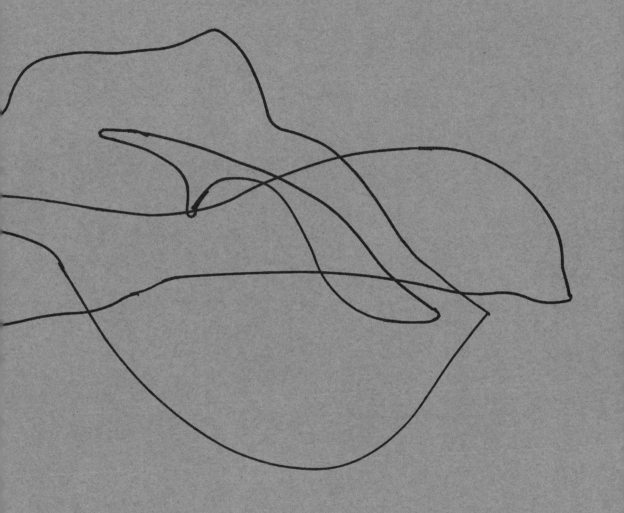

The Absence Factor

'How to deal with this terrifying poverty of abundance? My favourite solution is a test called the Absence Factor. It was devised by Jeremy Bullmore, one-time chairman of the J Walter Thompson advertising agency. It is very simple and deadly accurate.

'You consider any object and give it a value from zero to a hundred, depending on your estimate of how much you would miss it in a crisis. Thus, a gold harp in a drawing room, or indeed a De Longhi deep-fat fryer, scores very low while a loo roll, if in dire need on, say, a train in Gujarat, scores very nearly the maximum possible points. Simple pleasures rarely disappoint.'

Stephen Bayley
The Independent on Sunday, 14 March 2004

A matter of style

'You and I,' said Henri Rousseau at a celebratory dinner and addressing his host Pablo Picasso, 'are the two most important artists of the age – you in the Egyptian style, and I in the modern one.'

A Nomad Eye

I have a penchant for scenarios that juggle
with the natural order of things. Sometimes
one discerns an incongruous situation which
is usually camouflaged by common sense.
If I spot one, my first move is to put it down
on paper before it gets forgotten.

Assume you're lying on a beach. You're bored
and to entertain yourself you play a game of
mental sightseeing. You float your nomad eye
high above ground, move it around, look down,
look behind things, and look back at yourself.

The two eyes perceive, the third eye divines, the
mind's eye composes, the nomad eye explores.

Not many people know they have one.

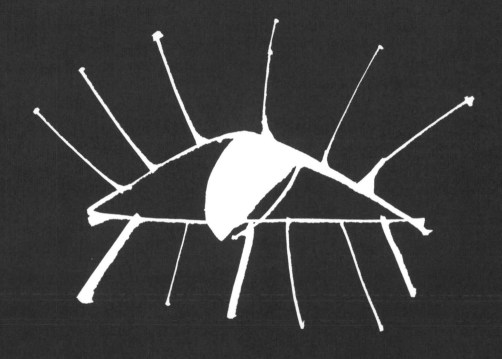

Shadow portraits

You probably remember from Peter Pan that a shadow belongs to a person as much as their face does. Furthermore, shadows change according to dress, location, season, and time of day. No two shadows are ever the same.

Your shadow is the essence of you at one moment in time.

I find my shadows in the photocopying machine. Ensure it is well primed in ink, open the lid – leave it open – and press a button. The machine delivers a rich deep carbon-black sheet of paper. Perforate around the edges of the drawing of the silhouette with a pin.

Carefully tear to realize the shadow.

By the way, did you know that the grayling butterfly tilts its wings to align with the sun so that it doesn't cast a shadow?

Self portrait
Sun behind
me. 12.15pm
24/VII/98
Castel d'Argile

Sarah facing
to my right.
12·25ᵖm. London
24/VII/98

Tobia
12:45 pm
16 September
Rethymnon
2004.

Streetscapes

What's under your nose often gets overlooked, although it may be more interesting than what's in front of it.

Take street markers. These aren't vague marks but significant symbols. Misinterpretation could be terminal. Yet they are a vocabulary which few comprehend except the bureaucrats who invented them.

Paradoxically they become abstractions which mean something.

Street markings, Pembridge Road, Notting Hill, London

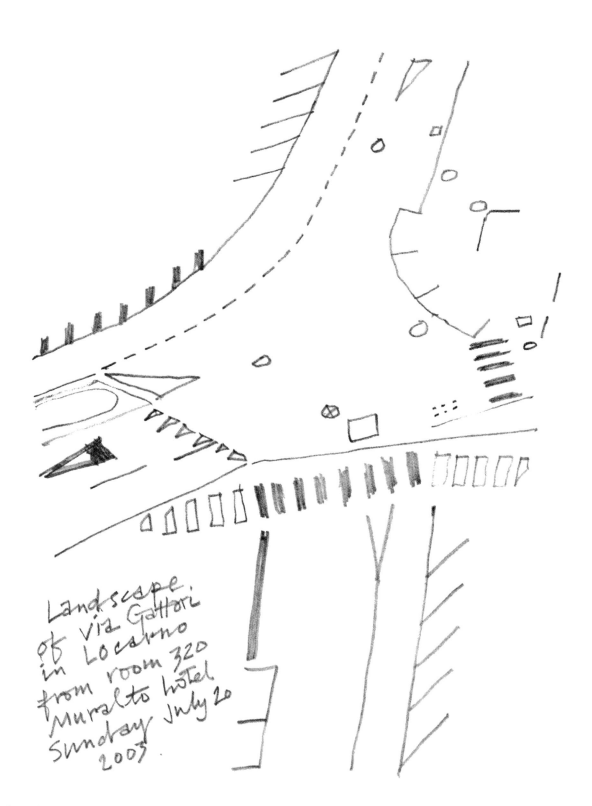

Landscape
of via Gattori
in Locarno
from room 320
Muralto hotel
Sunday July 20
2003

Drawn from room 320, Muralto Hotel, Locarno

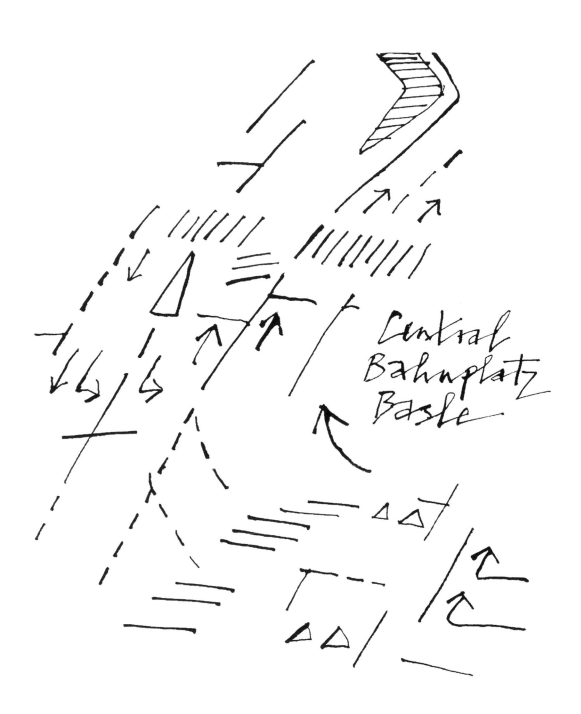

Central
Bahnplatz
Basle

Drawn from room 409, Hilton Hotel, Basle, 27 September 2002

Sunrises

During reflective moments on vacations
I sometimes make sunrises. An attempt to
capture that moment when the sun suddenly
arrives, like a cork popping out of a bottle.

The method is to brush in a stroke of colour –
this is the sea – then rapidly daub a disc
just above, so it touches the edge of the sea.
Whoomf. It's sudden death. It works or it
doesn't. It's a chancy business.

I do the sunrises over a drink in the evening.

Mindscaping

By looking at a scene in a certain way, a palm tree in the foreground can be aligned with one in the background. By mentally squashing space, the smaller palm below seems to be propping up the larger.

Overleaf the horizon ignores the lack of depth altogether and adjusts to fit the tree.

Three possible impossible realities.

'The fox knows many tricks; the hedgehog
one good one.'

Archilochus
Quoted by Aristotle in *Politics*

Sesquipedalianism

Hypnopompic : John Fowles, author of *The French Lieutenant's Woman* and *The Magus,* liked the semi-conscious haze between slumber and waking. The period when the sights and sounds of dreams still hover within reach and can be captured. It was while in this state that the plots and scenes of his novels revealed themselves to him. He called it his hypnopompic state.

Anagnorisis : This clumsy word defines that moment of discovery that forms the thin blue line between knowledge and ignorance – the whammo factor – the denouement in a drama – the moment you get it.

Ekphrasis : Ekphrasis is verbal representation of a visual representation – the description of an artwork. In ekphrasis, words give an impression of the picture; the picture gives an image of the world.

Floccinaucinihilipilification: the action of estimating as worthless.

Zyxt: The last entry in the twelve weighty volumes of the *Oxford English Dictionary*, which define 414,845 words, is this old Kentish word meaning to see.

Writing is Drawing

The Ancient Greeks had only one word for
writing and drawing, and that was *graphein*,
which originally meant to scratch, scrape
or graze.

Writing is handled by most people like a
passage of bad driving by a juvenile delinquent.
A thoughtless rush of scrawl across a sheet
of paper. A matter to be despatched as quickly
as possible.

Writing is not a pain in the neck. Writing is
the mind tracking out messages, thoughts
and feelings.

This collection of thoughts on thinking were
done with the same dip pen. The thicks
and thins of the strokes arriving by how one
used the pen.

Writing is you on paper.

Sometimes I am, sometimes I think.

We think in generalities, we live in detail.

Alfred North Whitehead

Life consists in what a man is THINKING all day.

DOGMA does not mean the absence of thought, but the end of thought.

Thinking is more interesting than knowing, but less interesting than looking.

Our
heads
are bound
to allow
our
thoughts
to change
direction.

Francis Picabia
279

A CONCLUSION is the place where you get tired of thinking

Greengrocer calligraphy seen and photographed by Leah Klein in Berwick Street market, Shepherd's Bush market, Portobello market, and

in stalls on Oxford Street and Goodge Street. Did they all go to the same school, I wonder?

The Twin Towers

I was in midtown Manhattan on that Tuesday.

In the streets people looked bewildered,
confused and stunned. Black smoke blanketed
the view looking south down the avenues.
Streets were deserted of traffic. There was an
acrid smell. It was hot.

Tourists (shorts, sandals, aloha shirts) uncertain
what to do, were wandering aimlessly taking
pictures of each other.

Shops, galleries, museums were closed, so
I trawled the street kiosks and bought every
postcard I could find that showed the twin
towers. I discovered some 30 different views.

These commemorate that day.

New York
11 September 2001:
At 2.45 pm I closed
my eyes and
strolled across 5th
Avenue.

AVENUE ROAD

← Pink Green

DUCKS WALK

Borough of Chelsea
TITE STREET
S.W.3

LONG
ACRE WC2
CITY OF WESTMINSTER

BOROUGH OF ISLINGTON
QUICK
STREET N.I

THE
PAVEMENT.S

OVAL WAY
SE11

THE CUT
SE1
SOUTH BANK

BOROUGH OF SOUTHWARK
SHORT ST.
S.E.I

London Borough of Hounslow
SWIFT ROAD
Hanw

CITY OF LONDON
CLOTH ST.
EC1

Street names seen and photographed by Harry Pearce.

FRIENDLY PLACE

VANE STREET SW1
CITY OF WESTMINSTER

DOWN ROAD

LONG WALK SE1
LONDON BOROUGH OF SOUTHWARK

LION CLOSE SE4

GOTHIC ROAD
Twickenham

PAYNE STREET SE8

LONDON BOROUGH OF ISLINGTON
OLD STREET E.C.I

CITY OF LONDON

SILK STREET EC2

CREEK ROAD SE8

CHANCE ST

BRIEF STREET
SE5

Facading

These facades were constructed with a variety of pens and pencils on various papers by different methods. Dip pens, rollerballs, ballpoints, fibre tips, soft pencils, hard leads. Coarse cartridge, smooth cold press, handmade papers, laid and wove stock, blotting paper.

The intention was to employ all sorts of materials and tools yet use them within limited constraints.

For example drawing a facade upside down, or back to front, or with the left hand, really concentrates the mind.

The buildings were loosely copied from postcards, photographs, travel books and other visual references. No travel expenditure, no problems with inclement weather.

The objective was to reverse the architectural process by reducing volume to line, to convert three dimensions into two. In other words, to flatten space.

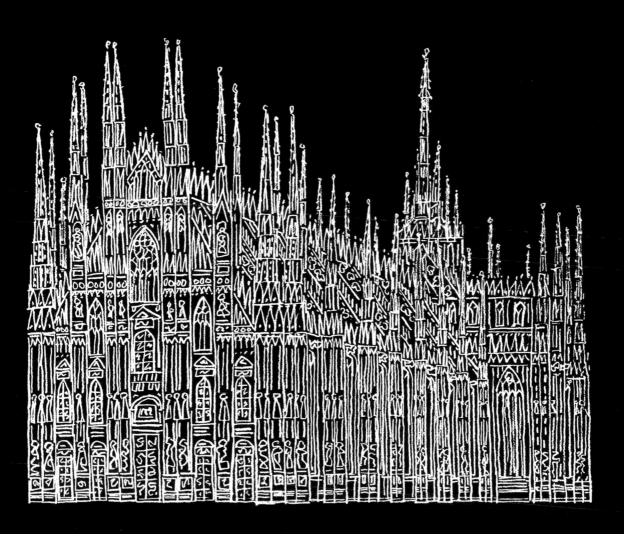

Il Duomo, Milan

San Miniato, Florence

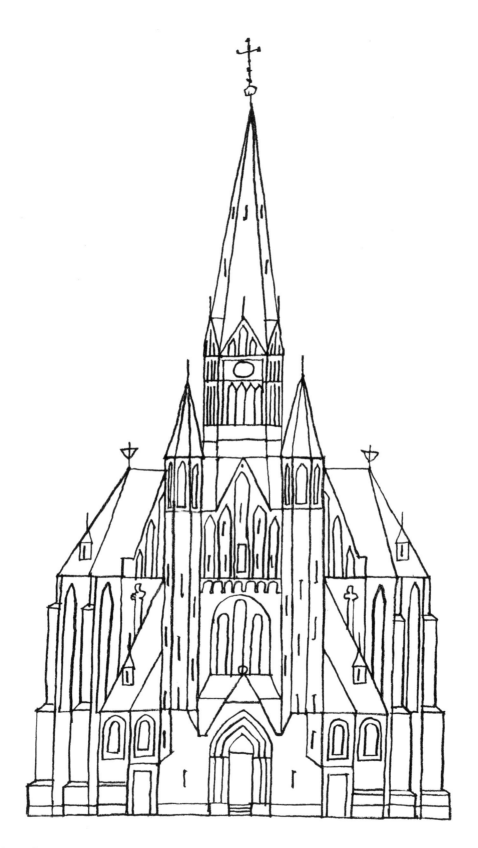

Vondelkerk, Amsterdam

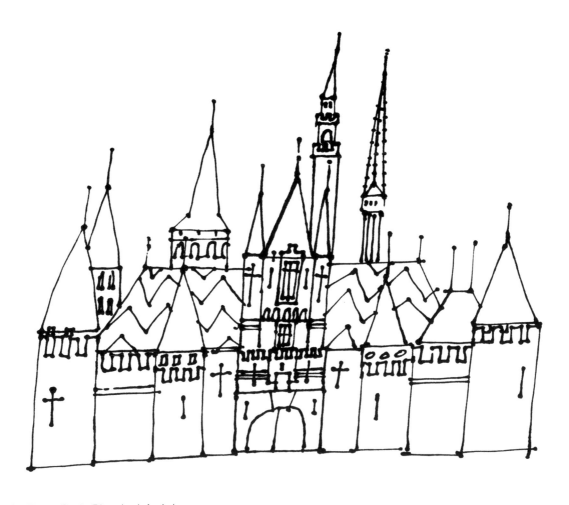

Sleeping Beauty Castle, Disneyland, Anaheim

Igreja do Carmo, Faro

297

Chrysler Building, New York
298

Horse Guards, London

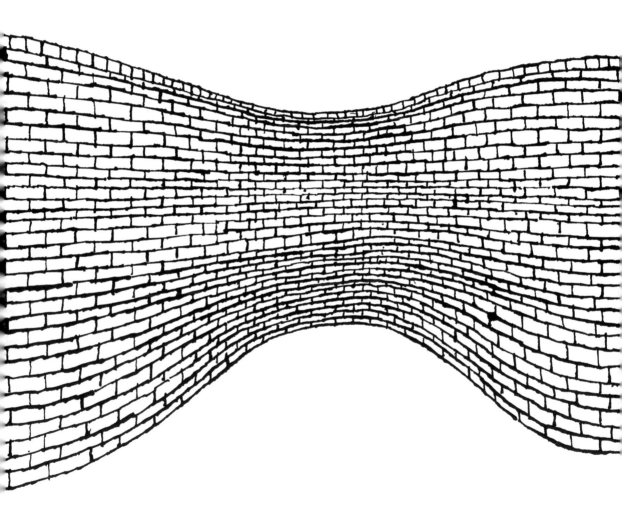

Crinkle-crankle wall, Suffolk. (The curves give the wall strength and enable it to be built high only a brick thick.)

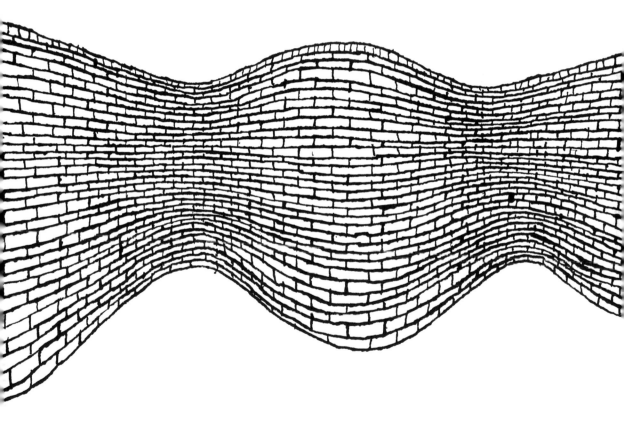

Sant'Agostino, Rome

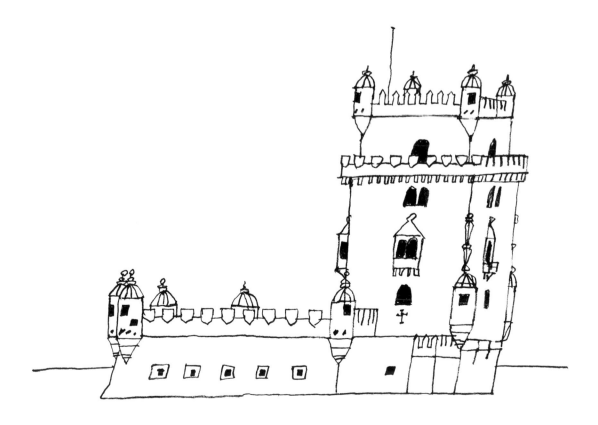

Torre de Belém, Lisbon

Nuraghi, Alghero

Santa Maria Novella, Florence
305

Krac des Chevaliers, Levant

Palazzo della Signoria, Florence

Gravestones, St Thomas Church, Winchelsea

Dorothy Parker, in her first job at *Vanity Fair* in New York, felt lonely sitting alone in her small office. In desperation she got a signwriter to letter out M E N on her office door.

Rooms

I read somewhere or other that cupboard 55 at
the British Museum holds the world's greatest
collection of erotic materials from antiquity.
On a recent visit I asked the information desk
in which room the cupboard was housed.
Fixing me with a what's-a-nasty-old-man-like-
you-want-to-know-for look, the twin-pearled
bat behind the desk told me I'd have to put
my enquiry in a letter. I didn't.

During his stay in London, Monet made
sketches and paintings of the bridges over
the Thames at Charing Cross and Waterloo.
He stayed in rooms 508 and 509 at the Savoy
Hotel. Both with good views of the river.

In 1926 Agatha Christie spent 11 days hard
at work in room 411 at the Pera Palas Hotel
in Istanbul. It was here that she drafted the
Byzantine plot of *Murder on the Orient Express*.

During the Second World War transmissions
from the German Enigma machine were
decoded by the boffins at Bletchley Park. They
were then sent to London and analysed for
action in room 40 at the Admiralty.

Hitler's bathroom

Flapper, model, Surrealist muse, ex-lover of Man Ray and war photographer, Lee Miller sat naked in Hitler's bath in his abandoned Munich apartment. David E Scherman, her then boyfriend, took the photograph. She took a matching photograph of David but you don't see that one so often.

The boots on the mat are a significant part of the story around this picture. That same morning Lee and David had visited Dachau, so the mat on which the boots are placed is dirty from the dust of the concentration camp, and Lee is in Hitler's bath cleansing herself of the horrors she had witnessed that day.

Room 606

'In the centre of Copenhagen, on the sixth floor of the SAS Royal Hotel, a single room preserves in microcosm the definitive masterwork of Arne Jacobsen. Room 606 is the last surviving interior of the SAS House, a lost world of abstract form and natural experience that was an unparalleled example of twentieth-century Scandinavian architecture and design.

'This monumental building provided Jacobsen with the opportunity to exercise the full range of the talents that have distinguished him as one of the twentieth century's most complex and versatile architects.

'He designed every detail of the building and the interiors, from the twenty-two-storey hotel tower to furniture, lighting, and textiles to the flatware for the hotel restaurant.'

Michael Sheridan
Room 606, Phaidon Press (London 2003)

Room 101

In his book *1984* George Orwell wrote that room 101 was 'the place where the worst thing that can happen to you – happens to you'. Room 101 was in Broadcasting House in Portland Place, where he wrote most of *1984* in the slack intervals between his broadcasting sessions.

The room was recently demolished as part of redevelopment and the BBC asked the sculptor Rachel Whiteread to commemorate the space. Whiteread is known for her 'negative' casts of objects from bathtubs to the inside of a Victorian terraced house.

She made a cast of the inside of room 101. There is a door on one side and two latticed windows on another; and on its surface there are abrasions and scarring where the pipes, vents and dado were pulled off the walls. The negative expression of the space, so to speak.

Gravy Williams

In a sense one might describe these illustrations as graphic nicknames.

Reversing a number 3 to create the letter E in JENNIE. The play on letters combining an ampersand (&) with the letter E to give ANDY, and the letters L and N for ELLEN.

Not quite the visual equivalents to Dicky Bird or Chalky White, but more akin to someone I heard introduced as Gravy Williams. Why 'gravy' someone else asked. 'Because he goes with anything,' said his friend.

HU as IC. Monogram for Ivan Chermayeff

ME as WF. Monogram for Willy Fleckhaus

Proportion

'It is important to realise that if three actors are on the stage together and two of them have a dialogue which the audience can accept as the third not overhearing, then the space must be sufficiently wide to allow this, without of course, depriving the audience's sense of intimacy. It is a matter of careful proportion.'

Alec Guinness
Blessings in Disguise, Hamish Hamilton (London 1985)

Real celebrities

Reading Bill Bryson's *A Short History of Nearly Everything*, I gradually became conscious of the whacky names that peopled the pages. Here are a few: Fritz Zwicky, Yakir Aharanov, Edson Bastin, Wayne Biddle, Annie Jump Cannon, Erwin Chargaffe, Glen Izett, Sharon Bertsch McGrayne, Corneille de Pauw, Caspar Witsar, Vesto Slipher.

On reflection, I don't see why I should have been so surprised. After all, the winner of the National Scrabble Championship held in London during 2004 was a Mr Harshan Lamabadusuriya.

Characterization

Letters are not only units to construct words, but also characters in their own right. Stiff, formal, simple, entertaining, etc.

They can also express actions, situations, places and feelings.

Word domains

The meaning of a word can be amplified by its letters. VENICE and MANHATTAN are not only words for specific places, but can visually represent those places.

Here are some word domains. If the citizens want to complain, let them eat cake.

ΛΕΝΙCΕ

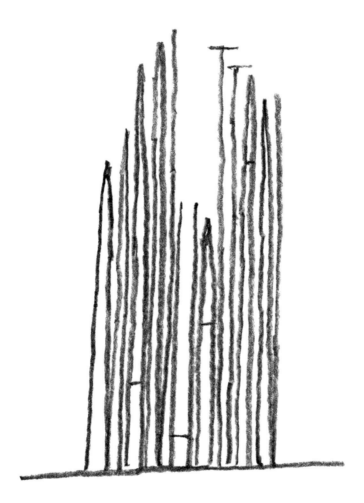

view driving in
from the
Triboro bridge

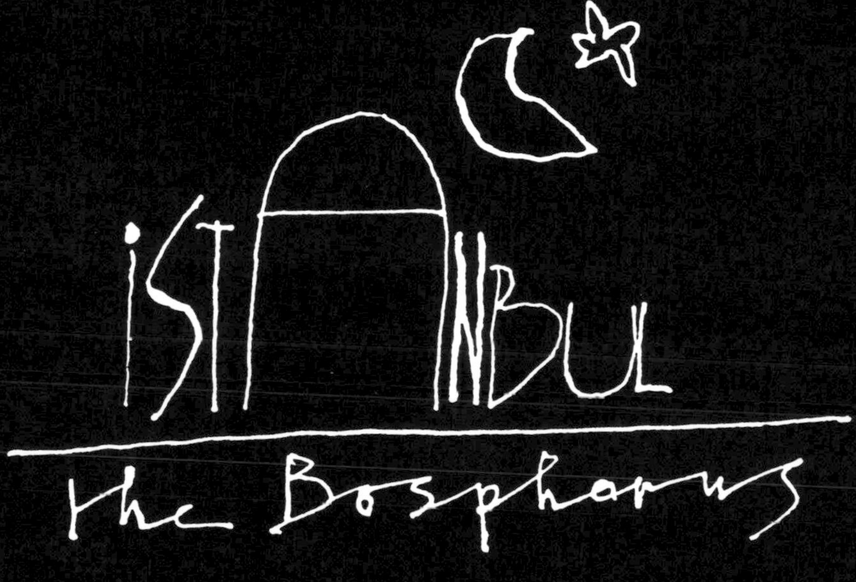
iSTANBUL
the Bosphorus

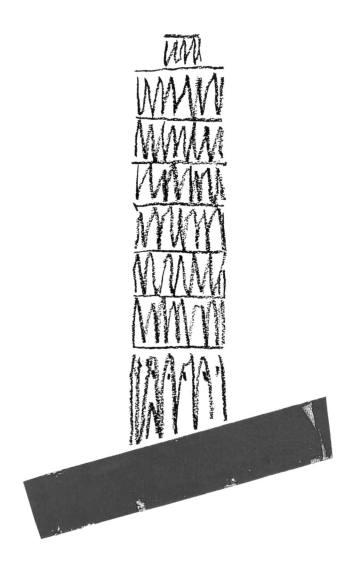

Fred Astaire was known for his fantastic elaborate dance routines. But real credit to his partner Ginger Rogers – who did the same routine backwards and in high heels.

Make believe

'I went to Las Vegas for the first time to participate in the AIGA conference. I was booked at the Venetian – a hotel whose vast vistas of painted, cloud-filled skies had required the skills of more mural painters than existed in Venice during the entire fifteenth century.

'On my first day at the hotel, I noticed a sign that said "Grand Canal," I asked the concierge at the reception desk where it was. "One flight up", she said. The earth reeled beneath my feet. A canal one flight up; what a concept.

'The canal was, in fact, upstairs, complete with gondola and gondolier who would cheerfully take you around the bend to the Piazza San Marco. Later that same day, the hotel's plumbing broke down, and suddenly the entire ground floor began to smell like Venice on a warm day. I actually found myself wondering whether the hotel had planned it. Is there such a thing as a virtual smell?'

Milton Glaser
AIGA Voice Conference, Washinton, DC, 23 March 2002

Letterworks

In the West we have little regard for writing. And indeed many people are even proud they have a bad (aka lazy) hand. Personally I abhor sloppy writing. It conveys there's something dodgy about the writer's personal hygiene, ethical values, and emotional shortfall. Fancy not enjoying the sensuous pleasure in the penning of a thought.

At art school I was taught by two distinguished calligraphers. One was a lady who'd spent ten years lettering out the names of all the pilots killed during the Battle of Britain in the *Book of Remembrance*. The other was a fellow who wore an embroidered smock and was extremely highly strung – after all, a slip of the pen can ruin months of work. Most people respond to skilled calligraphy with admiration.

I think most calligraphy is boringly manicured, on the other hand I'm attracted to anarchic handwriting. The difference is one of attitude. Calligraphers generally have too much respect for skill at the expense of expression.

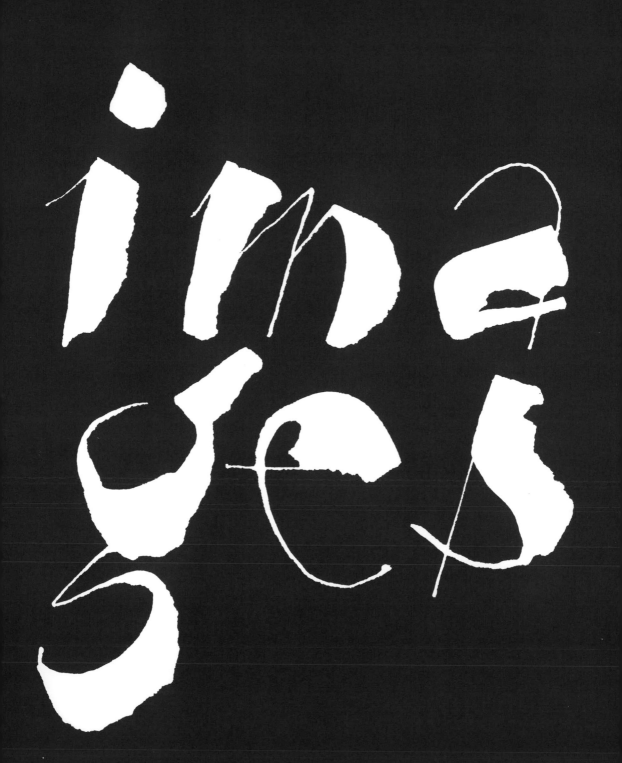

Calligraphic bricolage

The *bricole* was a medieval military machine for throwing stones. Nowadays the term refers to a shot in billiards which doesn't turn out as intended but is nevertheless reasonably successful.

I received an invitation to participate in the Ink Painting Biennial held in Shenzhen, China.

In due course an immense parcel arrived. About a hundred sheets of paper, a brush as large as a broom, sticks of solid ink and a substantial heavy slate palette.

I sensed I was in deep trouble.

Choice of subject was determined by lack of skill. Misty scenes of lakes and mountain peaks, bamboo rustling in the wind, or peasants toiling in paddy fields, were instantly dismissed.

I was left with calligraphy. Now the Chinese have been doing calligraphy for 5,000 years and I only had a month. I'm not a calligrapher but was prepared to settle for vigorous hand-writing. Even this posed a problem. The paper was singularly absorbent and the ink spread instantly as soon as brush touched paper.

Faced with an uncontrollable situation I relied on spontaneity and luck.

Adolf Loos
343

Typographic melange

These designs appeared on the covers of the English-language and foreign-language editions of *The Children's Art Book* published by Phaidon.

The letters were cut freehand out of coloured papers. The counters – the holes in letters – were treated as solids and given their own colour.

The intention was to create similarity of appearance even though the language and number of words varied with the editions.

Sort of an exercise in reverse engineering.

IL MONDO DELL'ARTE PER RAGAZZI

Memos from Gozo

Gozo is a smaller island off the small island of Malta. A long time ago this is where I spent a lazy summer month.

Between swimming, eating, sleeping and reading, I constructed drawn observations and thoughts about Ggantija. This is the oldest known stone structure in Europe and for some mysterious reason, it is located on this tiny Mediterranean island.

Anyway, assembling lines and organizing fragments and so forth for the temples, soon extended into comments about the weather, mood and place of the island.

By constructed I mean that each line of an overlapped letter was drawn independently of the line that preceded or followed it. Thus there are no continuous lines as no line physically crosses another (see detail overleaf).

Writing this explanation it occurs to me that someone might ask why go to all that trouble.

I don't know.

Coffee in Xlendi

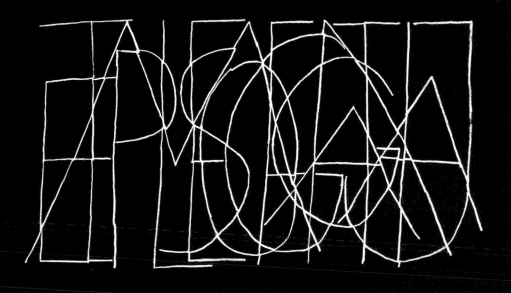

More Gozo

Each village has its own disproportionately enormous church and annual festive celebration. To mark the occasion, the church facades are peppered with tiny coloured lights in elaborate decorative patterns.

Unless it's an exceptionally clear night the lights and colours diffuse and intermingle to display a beautiful chromatic smudge.

An effect heightened – when it rains...

Festa in Xaghra

Anachronisms

The 0 in the number 10 on the black door
of the British prime minister's house at
10 Downing Street is wonky. Take a look
when you next see a newsreel.

Watching a film with Hugh Grant being
elected prime minister, I noticed the door as
he entered No.10. The 0 was dead symmetrical.
A convincing scene but just a clever set.

According to designer Michael Bierut, the
dials on the pressure gauges of the *Titanic*, in
the movie, are rendered in a typeface called
Helvetica. That, to a typographic enthusiast,
is really laughable. Helvetica was designed in
1957 and the *Titanic* went down in 1912.

Now Michael must have a sharp eye for such
details. Perhaps a talent engendered by being
born with a name with a spelling error.

This is a typeface

'A typeface customarily has two hundred
and twenty eight characters, including letters,
accents, numerals, fractions, ligatures (the
structures that in certain faces join letters
together); commercial signs, such as those
for the dollar and the euro; and punctuation
marks, ampersands, and peculiars, such as
asterisks and daggers for footnotes.

'A type designer typically produces four
versions of a face: roman – that is, upright
letters – italic, bold roman, and bold italic.

'Such a grouping is called a family.'

Alec Wilkinson
The New Yorker, 5 December 2005

An Alphabet of Sorts

These collages are individual letters garnered from different sources and utilized to create new letters by judicious combinations.

The endeavour is to create an alphabet of 26 letters in which each letter will be constructed from two other kinds of letter. I suppose one might think of it as an alphabet of 78 letters.

Anyway, here are eight candidates from work in progress.

Such typographic miscegenation serves no functional purpose. That might explain why I enjoy making the letters.

B + R = B
361

O + O = O
362

B + T = P

P + K = R
364

O + O = S
365

J + U = S
367

V + V = X

368

R, or Block R	**Running R**	**Walking R**	**Flying 8**
Drag R	**Tumbling R**	**Lazy R**	**Bench 5**
Reverse R	**Crazy R**	**Barbed, or Jag R**	**Seventy-Six**
Rocking R	**R Quarter Circle**	**Swinging R**	**Fifty-Two**
Quarter Circle R	**Circle R**	**Box R**	**Slash Lazy Y**
Bench R	**Half Diamond R**	**Rafter R**	**Circle**
Bar R	**Bar R**	**R Bar**	**Half Circle J**
R Bar	**Diamond R**	**Slash R**	**Sun**

LAZY 2	ROCKING 6	LAZY HEART	CRAZY HEART
ROCKING 7	TUMBLING 4	RUNNING A	RUNNING B
SIXTY-THREE	NINETY-SIX	RUNNING N	RUNNING R
FORTY-FOUR	SEVENTY-FIVE	RUNNING W	RUNNING Y
		CRAZY R	CRAZY F
BAR M	BAR B Q		
MASHED CIRCLE, OR GOOSE EGG	QUARTER CIRCLE	I SEE YOU	I BAR YOU
HALF MOON	QUARTER MOON	BARKER	BARKEY
BUCKLE	HEART	KENO	SEVEN UP

Bits and pieces

This is a composition of the bits I would
normally throw away after I've utilized the
bits of bits other people have thrown away.

Randomly assembled and stuck down with
no objective in mind this work says and
means nothing.

What a relief.

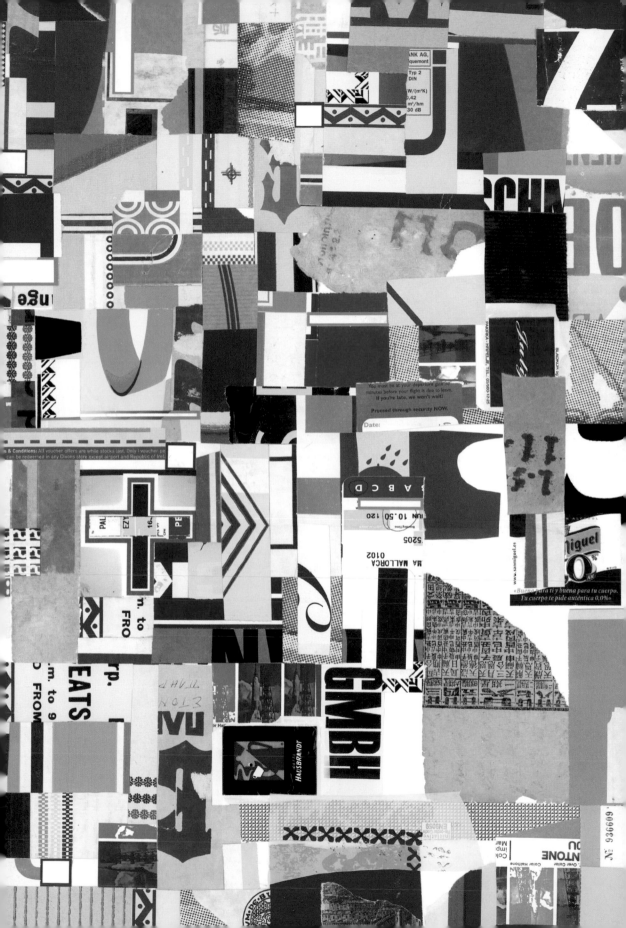

'Outside of a dog, a book is a man's best friend: and inside a dog, it's too dark to read.'

Groucho Marx

Illustration Credits:

All images, illustrations and calligraphy are
courtesy of the author, except for photography by:
Zafer Baran: 045–056
Ron Burton/Getty Images: 010
Nigel Haynes: 061
Primŏz Korŏsec: opening page
Harry Pearce: 290–291
Andrew Reeves: 254
François Robert: 170–171
Ralph Selby: 179
David E Scherman: 312–313
©Lee Miller Archives, England 2006.
All rights reserved. www.leemiller.co.uk

Author's acknowledgements:

I thank: Jean Robert for his faces; Harry Pearce
for his streets; Ron Arad, for lending his Marylin
curves; Sarah Copplestone, Leah Klein,
Paola and Raffaella Fletcher; and at Phaidon
Press, Diego García Scaro, Paul Hammond,
Amanda Renshaw, Richard Schlagman and
Emilia Terragni.

I also thank the following for their contributions:

Atelier Works: 090–091
Baseline magazine: 193–215
Black Sun: 274–280
Chartered Society of Designers: 216
Graphique magazine: 101
The Paul Hamlyn Foundation: 329
Icograda: 341
ISTD Fine Paper Limited: 121–128
Jaguar Cars Limited: 154
Monographica: 013–020, 026–040
Notting Hill Gate Improvements Group: 025
Novartis Campus: 102–105
Parker Pen: 100
Pentagram and G+B Arts: 137–148, 233–244
Roger Taylor: 067–071
UNESCO, RSA and Design Museum: 112–116

Phaidon Press Limited
Regent's Wharf
All Saints Street
London N1 9PA

Phaidon Press Inc.
180 Varick Street
New York, NY 10014

First published 2006
©2006 Phaidon Press Limited

ISBN-10: 0 7148 4712 7
ISBN-13: 978 0 7148 4712 2

A CIP catalogue of this
book is available from
the British Library.

Design by Alan Fletcher
Printed in Hong Kong

To learn more about Phaidon,
to keep up to date with
our publications, to sign up
to receive our newsletter,
and to benefit from special
promotions, visit us at
www.phaidon.com

ISBN 0-7148-4712-7
ISBN 978-0-7148-4712-2

9 780714 847122